Sheep

by Peter Brady

W
FRANKLIN WATTS
NEW YORK • LONDON • SYDNEY

This edition first published in 1998

Franklin Watts
96 Leonard Street
London EC2A 4RH

Franklin Watts Australia
14 Mars Road
Lane Cove
NSW 2066

Original edition published in the United States by Capstone Press
818 North Willow Street, Mankato, Minnesota 56001
Copyright © 1996, 1998 by Capstone Press

ISBN 0 7496 3203 8
Dewey Decimal Classification Number: 636.3

A CIP catalogue record for this book is available from the British Library.

Printed in Belgium

Photographs
All the photographs were taken by William Muñoz, except for the picture on page 10
which was taken by Peter Ford.

Contents

Words in the text in **bold** type are explained in the Useful words section on page 23.

What is a sheep?

A sheep is a farm animal.
Sheep are reared for their meat and wool.
Male sheep are called rams,
and female sheep are called ewes
(which sounds like 'yoos').

What sheep look like

Sheep have broad shoulders,
heavy bodies and short legs.
Their wool can be long and shaggy
or short and curly.
Sheep can be black, white,
brown, grey or spotted.

Where sheep live

Sheep are farm animals.
Different **breeds** live on farms
in different parts of the country.
Sheep have woollen coats
that are waterproof
so they can be outside all year round.

What sheep eat

Sheep mostly eat grass.
Sometimes they are put into fields
at harvest time to graze on **stubble**.
Sheep have no top front teeth.
At first they swallow the grass,
then they bring it up again later
to chew.

Different kinds of sheep

Farmers have kept sheep
for hundreds of years.
Now there are more than
800 different breeds.
The names of some of them are
Angora, Dorset, Hampshire,
Nubian and Southdown.
Some sheep even have horns.

Shearing

Sheep grow thick wool coats
to keep them warm in winter.
In late spring or early summer
the wool is sheared.
The wool is cut off all in one piece.
Wool from one sheep is called a **fleece**.
A fleece can weigh
between 1.5 and 9 kilos.

Bleating

When a lamb is born
one of the first things it hears
is its mother's **bleat**.
The lamb bleats back.
The ewe and lamb
will recognize each other's bleat
for the rest of their lives.

Lambs

Ewes usually give birth to two lambs
early in the spring.
If the weather is bad,
lambs are kept indoors.
Lambs are frisky and playful,
but stay close to their mothers
when they are very young.

What sheep give us

Sheep give us the wool
to make clothes, blankets, and
furnishings such as carpets and rugs.
Sheepskin is made into leather
for gloves and shoes.
Meat from sheep is an important food,
and ewes' milk is also used
to make cheese.

How to spin wool

Before fleece can be made into cloth it must be spun into woollen thread. You can learn to do this without having a sheep!

What you need
> Good supply of cotton wool

What you do
1   Hold the ball of cotton wool between your thumb and first finger.
2   With the other hand pinch a little of the cotton wool and slowly pull it away from the rest of the ball. Twist the cotton wool as you pull it.
3   Continue doing this until you have a nice long thread.

The thread should be strong and smooth. If the thread is lumpy, you need to pull it out more. If the thread breaks very easily, you need to twist it more tightly.

Useful words

bleat the cry of a sheep

breed group of animals with the same ancestors

fleece the coat of a sheep after it has been sheared off

stubble the short stalks left in fields after the crops have been cut

waterproof something that stops water getting through

Books to read

Dineen, Jacqueline, *Farms,* Macdonald 1985

First Discovery: Farm Animals, Moonlight Publishing, 1996

See How They Grow: Lamb, Dorling Kindersley, 1992

Whitlock, Ralph, *Sheep*, Wayland, 1982

Index

PRINTED IN BELGIUM BY
proost
INTERNATIONAL BOOK PRODUCTION